EARLY PHYSICS FUN
PAPER
AIRPLANES

by Jenny Fretland VanVoorst

pogo

Ideas for Parents and Teachers

Pogo Books let children practice reading informational text while introducing them to nonfiction features such as headings, labels, sidebars, maps, and diagrams, as well as a table of contents, glossary, and index.

Carefully leveled text with a strong photo match offers early fluent readers the support they need to succeed.

Before Reading

- "Walk" through the book and point out the various nonfiction features. Ask the student what purpose each feature serves.

- Look at the glossary together. Read and discuss the words.

Read the Book

- Have the child read the book independently.

- Invite him or her to list questions that arise from reading.

After Reading

- Discuss the child's questions. Talk about how he or she might find answers to those questions.

- Prompt the child to think more. Ask: Have you ever made a paper airplane? What design did you use? How do you think your design affected the way the plane flew?

Pogo Books are published by Jump!
5357 Penn Avenue South
Minneapolis, MN 55419
www.jumplibrary.com

Library of Congress Cataloging-in-Publication Data

Names: Fretland VanVoorst, Jenny, 1972- author.
Title: Paper airplanes / by Jenny Fretland VanVoorst.
Description: Minneapolis, MN: Jump! Inc., [2016] |
Series: Early physics fun | Audience: Ages 7-10.
Identifiers: LCCN 2015039090 | ISBN 9781620313176 (hardcover: alk. paper) | ISBN 9781624963698 (ebook)
Subjects: LCSH: Paper airplanes—Design and construction—Juvenile literature. | Aerodynamics—Juvenile literature. | Physics—Study and teaching (Elementary)—Juvenile literature.
Classification: LCC TL778.F74 2016 | DDC 533.62—dc23
LC record available at http://lccn.loc.gov/2015039090

Series Designer: Anna Peterson
Photo Researcher: Anna Peterson

Photo Credits: All photos by Shutterstock except: Corbis, 5; Dreamstime, 4, 12-13; Getty, 8-9; iStock, 6-7; Thinkstock, 10-11.

Printed in the United States of America at Corporate Graphics in North Mankato, Minnesota.

TABLE OF CONTENTS

CHAPTER 1

AERODYNAMIC FORCES

Paper airplanes are easy and fun to make. They can also teach you a lot about **physics**.

What makes your airplane soar or drop? How do the wings affect its flight?

Physics is the science of matter and how it moves. Like all sciences, there are physics **laws** by which all things operate. Even paper airplanes!

Understand the physics of flight, and you can turn an ordinary piece of paper into an amazing flying machine!

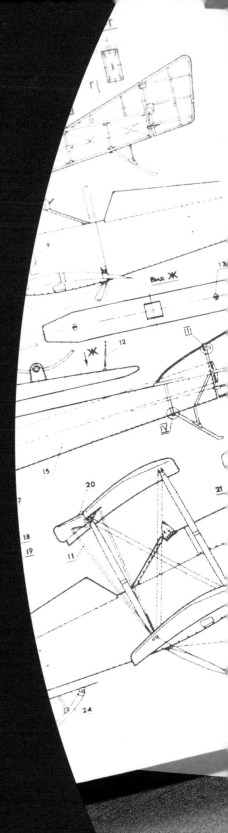

Have you ever built and thrown a paper airplane? If so, you'll know that different designs cause planes to fly differently. An airplane's design affects its **aerodynamics**. It determines how far a plane can fly. It determines the amount of time it can spend in the air.

There are four **forces** that act on an airplane. When these four forces are used in balance, the paper airplane will fly longer.

DID YOU KNOW?

The world record for a paper airplane flight was set in 1998. It lasted 27.6 seconds!

CHAPTER 2

THRUST VS. DRAG

Thrust is the force that moves the plane forward.

With a paper airplane, this force comes from the throw. A strong throw gives a lot of thrust. A weak throw gives less thrust.

air particles

Drag

Thrust

Thrust

Drag

Thrust is balanced by **drag**. What is drag? As a plane glides through the air, tiny **particles** rub against it. These particles "drag" on the plane, slowing it down. This works against thrust. It reduces the plane's forward speed.

DID YOU KNOW?

The rough surface of a normal piece of paper can cause a lot of drag. **Origami paper** is great for building paper planes. Why? The paper is very smooth. This lets drag have less of an effect.

CHAPTER 3

LIFT VS. GRAVITY

Lift is the force that acts on the plane's wings to move it upward. How does lift work?

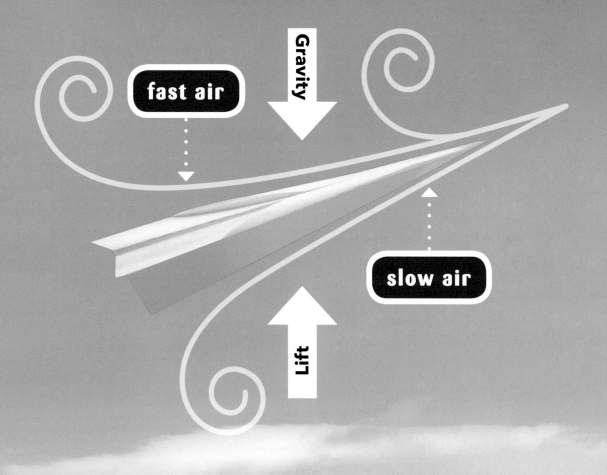

As a plane moves forward, the wing splits the air. The air that moves over the wing speeds up. The air below the wing, however, moves more slowly. This causes a difference in **pressure**. The pressure difference is what lifts the plane up.

Gravity is the force that works to balance lift. Gravity pulls the plane downward. It pulls it back to Earth. If gravity weren't acting on the plane, the plane would never fall. It would fly forever.

Gravity is the only force of the four that can't be changed.

Four forces act on a paper airplane.

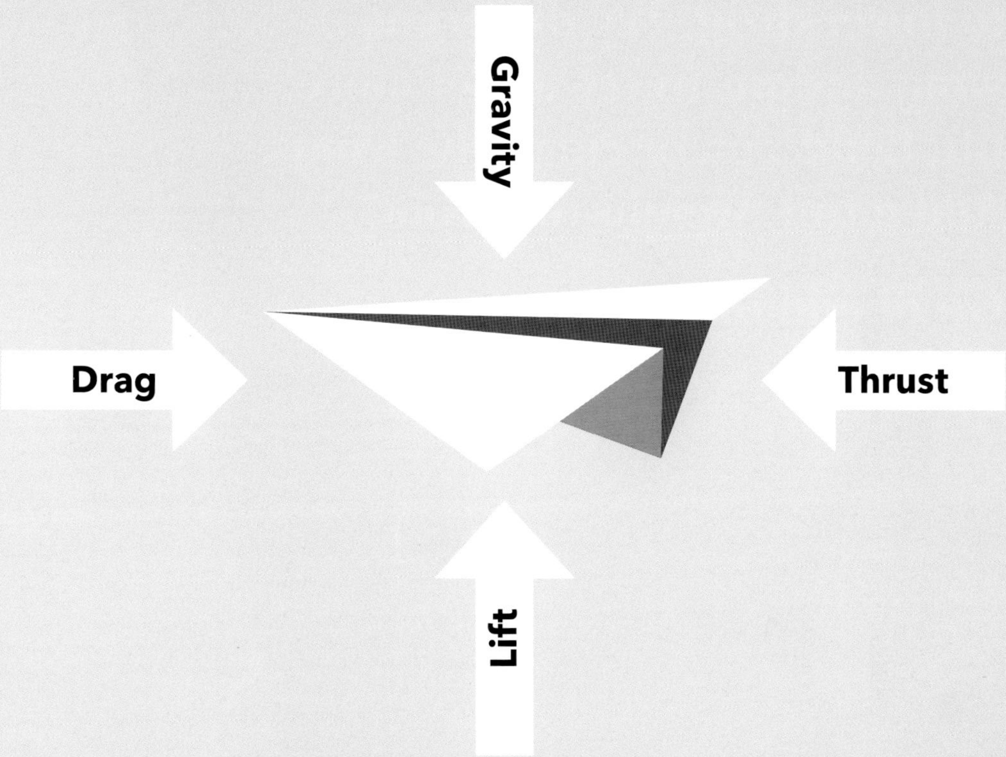

Gravity

Drag

Thrust

Lift

You can play with these forces to try to change your plane's flight. Throw harder for more thrust. Use smoother paper to lower drag. Try different wing designs to try to get more lift. Bend, cut, or curve the wings. Add a tail. Weight the front.

Go ahead and play with physics. It's fun!

ACTIVITIES & TOOLS

PAPER AIRPLANE FLIGHT TEST

There are many designs of paper airplanes. Some designs are good for distance, some for flight time, and some for accuracy. Let's look at different airplane designs to see how they compare. Use designs that you know of or find online.

1. Make all of the paper airplanes that you plan on using.

2. In an open area with plenty of room to fly, throw all of the planes and record the distance that they flew. Repeat this until you have 10 trials for each plane.

3. After you have finished with the distance tests, get a stopwatch to time the flights. Record the times and repeat until you have 10 trials for each plane.

4. To test accuracy, choose a target. Pick a launch spot and throw each plane 10 times at the target. Record the number of times that each plane hits the target.

5. Have an adult help you average your results. How do the results for each plane compare? Why do you think the best planes performed as well as they did?

GLOSSARY

aerodynamics: Relating to the movement of air and the forces acting on bodies exposed to it.

drag: The force acting on an airplane to slow it down as the body moves through the air.

force: An influence (as a push or pull) that tends to produce a change in the speed or direction of motion of something.

gravity: The attraction of the earth for bodies at or near its surface.

laws: Scientific rules.

lift: An upward force (as on an airplane wing) that opposes the pull of gravity.

origami paper: A special paper designed to be used for folding.

particles: Very small parts of matter.

physics: The area of science that has to do with matter and how it moves through space and time.

pressure: The force exerted as a result of the weight of the atmosphere.

thrust: The force, created by throwing, that drives a paper airplane forward.

INDEX

TO LEARN MORE

Learning more is as easy as 1, 2, 3.

1) Go to www.factsurfer.com

2) Enter "paperairplanes" into the search box.

3) Click the "Surf" button to see a list of websites.

With factsurfer, finding more information is just a click away.